This Journal Belongs To

_____

Date _____

WRITE IDEAS BLANK JOURNAL

Copyright © 1993
Brownlow Publishing Company, Inc.
6309 Airport Freeway / Fort Worth, Texas 76117

*Have a heart that never hardens,
and a temper that never tires,
and a touch that never hurts.*

CHARLES DICKENS

*You will find, as you look back upon your life,
that the moments when you really lived
are the moments when you have done things
in the spirit of love.*

HENRY DRUMMOND

*Delight yourself in the LORD
and he will give you
the desires of your heart.*

PSALM 37:4

*All of us desire peace, but very few
desire those things that make for peace.*

THOMAS A' KEMPIS

৪৯

*The Lord has done great things for us,
and we are filled with joy.*

PSALM 126:3

৪১

*Be a life long or short, its completeness
depends on what it was lived for.*

DAVID STARR JORDAN

৪৯

*So we fix our eyes not on what is seen,
but on what is unseen. For what is seen is temporary,
but what is unseen is eternal.*

2 CORINTHIANS 4:18

The only ones among you who will be really happy are those who will have sought and found how to serve.

ALBERT SCHWEITZER

*The grass withers and the flowers fall,
but the word of our God stands forever.*

ISAIAH 40:8

*I slept, and I dreamed that life was all joy.
I woke, and saw that life was but service.
I served, and discovered that service was joy.*

RABINDRANATH TAGORE

*In God I trust; I will not be afraid.
What can man do to me?*

PSALM 56:11

৪৯

*Wherever there is a human being,
there is an opportunity for kindness.*

SENECA

82

A single thought in the morning may fill our whole day with joy and sunshine or gloom and depression.

PARAMANANDA

*Were there no God we would be in this glorious world
with grateful hearts and no one to thank.*

CHRISTINA ROSSETTI

We are so very rich if we know just a few people in a way in which we know no other.

CATHERINE BRAMWELL-BOOTH

*Worry does not empty tomorrow of its sorrow;
it empties today of its strength.*

CORRIE TEN BOOM

*The Lord does not look at the things man looks at.
Man looks at the outward appearance,
but the Lord looks at the heart.*

1 SAMUEL 16:7

Those who would have nothing to do with thorns must never attempt to gather flowers.

There's only one corner of the universe you can be certain of improving, and that's your own self. So you have to begin there, not outside, not on other people. That comes afterwards, when you have worked on your own corner.
ALDOUS HUXLEY

૪૨

*The way to love anything
is to realize it might be lost.*
G. K. CHESTERTON

*I love the Lord, for he heard my voice; he heard my cry
for mercy. Because he turned his ear to me,
I will call on him as long as I live.*

PSALM 116:1,2

*No one has the right to look with contempt on himself
when God has shown such an interest in him.*

৪২

Your Father knows what you need before you ask him.

MATTHEW 6:8

Just as there are no little people or unimportant lives, there is no insignificant work.

ELENA BONNER

*And we know that in all things
God works for the good of those who love him.*

ROMANS 8:28

If life were predictable it would cease to be life and be without flavor.

ELEANOR ROOSEVELT

*To understand any living thing you must creep within
and feel the beating of its heart.*

W. MACNEILE DIXON

> *Do not have your concert first and tune your instruments afterward. Begin the day with God.*
>
> — JAMES HUDSON TAYLOR

*How great is the love the Father has lavished on us,
that we should be called children of God!*

1 JOHN 3:1

૪૭

The capacity to care gives life its deepest significance.
PABLO CASALS

૪૭

۴۹

The great acts of love are done by those who are habitually performing small acts of kindness.

*God loves us the way we are
but He loves us too much to leave us that way.*

LEIGHTON FORD

I will not forget you! See, I have engraved you on the palms of my hands.

ISAIAH 49:15,16

When we forget ourselves, we usually do something that everyone else remembers.

The cure for anything is salt water—sweat, tears, or the sea.
ISAK DINESEN

৪৩